American
Oak
Furniture

Kathryn McNerney

COLLECTOR BOOKS
A Division of Schroeder Publishing Co., Inc.

The current values in this book should be used only as a guide. They are not intended to set prices, which vary from one section of the country to another. Auction prices as well as dealer prices vary greatly and are affected by condition as well as demand. Neither the Author nor the Publisher assumes responsibility for any losses that might be incurred as a result of consulting this guide.

Searching For A Publisher?

We are always looking for knowledgeable people considered experts within their fields. If you feel there is a real need for a book on your collectible subject and have a large comprehensive collection, contact us.

COLLECTOR BOOKS
P.O BOX 3009
PADUCAH, KENTUCKY 42002-3009

Additional copies of this book may be ordered from:

Collector Books
P.O. Box 3009
Paducah, Kentucky 42002-3009

@ $9.95. Add $2.00 for postage and handling.

Copyright: Kathryn McNerney, 1984
Values Updated 1994

FOR GEORGE AND DOTTY FELLOWS

My Relatives...and...My Friends

Appreciation

To all those who touched my life as I was preparing this manuscript...permitted pictures, discussed the Oak and its furniture applications, just plain listened, wrote notes, and measured objects...or simply gave me infinite patience and tolerance...Thank You.

Alabama
The Spinning Wheel, Fairhope
Atchinson's Courtyard Antiques,
   Mobile

Florida
Dot's Early Times Antiques,
   Milton
Kathy and Rebecca McNerney
   Orange Park
The Country Cricket, Orange Park
Carl's Corner, Pensacola
Carol Piper, Pensacola
Commander Bill and Dee
   Faessel, Pensacola
Corley's Antiques, Pensacola
Daniels' Antiques, Pensacola
Dennis Sullivan's Antiques,
   Pensacola
Hamilton House, Pensacola
Mildred Lavespere, Pensacola
The Loft, Pensacola

Georgia
Kudzu Korner, Decatur

Kentucky
Bill and Meredith Schroeder,
   Paducah
Harry Shelton and Carolyn
   Lane, Wickliffe
Myrtle Scott, Wickliffe

Louisiana
Brown House Antiques,
   Lafayette

Missouri
Markland's Antique Shop,
   Armstrong
Dorothy Robb's Antiques,
   Moberly
Jim's Country Barn,
   Moberly

The Burtons, Moberly & Clark

New York
The Garrett, Buffalo
Lewiston Landing, Lewiston
Country Barn Shop, Wilson
Railroad Museum Association,
   Wilson
Grant and Nettie Martin,
   Youngstown
Old Fort Niagara Asociation,
   Youngstown
Sharon Fisher, Youngstown
Bruce and the Richard Smiths,
   Youngstown

North Carolina
Rachel's Antiques, Greenboro

Ohio
Mrs. Czar Allen, Columbus

Tennessee
Log Cabin Antiques, Carthage
Douglas and Marie Blair,
   Murfreesboro
Hope Vere-Anderson VII,
   Antiques,
Murfreesboro Antique Mall
   Management and Dealers,
   Murfreesboro
Sarah Endsley, Murfreesboro
The Rev. John and Mary
   Bowman, Murfreesboro
Bill and Joan Pace, Nashville
Collector's Choice, Nashville
Gene and Marie Norris, Smyrna

Virginia
Carlton and Vermell Cobb,
   Chesapeake

Canada
Rob and Ron VanRiel, Highland
   Antiques, Burlington, Ontario

Contents

Forest to Furniture

SOURCE

An apprehensive Acorn newly-swept from a massive arm of his White Oak parent hugged the earth under a dank mat of twigs and leaves. Unlike his Black (Red) Oak cousins who needed two years to mature, he could manage it in about one; that is, if he escaped squirrels and woods-rooting pigs, or being gathered by Indians who would pulverize, leach (to rid the bitter taste), and cook him as food! Though his kin numbered 300 species under the Beech Clan (Pin, Water, Holly, Spanish, Live, Bur, Willow, and Laurel among the hardwood trees and shrubs, and many more settled elsewhere in the world, while the tropical Cork Oak has commercial providence in North America), he determined to reach his own special destiny.

Musing on legendary tales sighed and rustled by his revered elders (and factual information he had overheard as woodsmen and hikers rested below him in the shade), he knew that since time began, Oaks were a symbol of strength, favored by the Norse god Thor, sacred to the Druids. Colonists hid their records in a "thousand years old" Charter Oak (standing until 1856 at Hartford, Connecticut) when their New England Governor General demanded those charter papers be surrendered.

In reality his bark and/or acorn cups might be used in medicines, as tanning for dyes and animals' hides; his lumber trod upon in lovely marks-resistant flooring; travel the oceans as ships' beams; provide handles for tools and casks for spirits (with White Oak the staves); converted into any number of things. Best of all, maybe he'd become tough, durable, handsome furniture (solid rather than veneer, since the latter was also lovely but secondary), and even achieve large protuberant burls for costly ornamentation.

WOODS

As sunlight paced the hours along, the Acorn gained confidence and pride of his potential. Flat-grained (or plain-sawed) logs cut in parallel layers beginning at the outer edge were excellent and in demand. If he could just grow extra-large around the middle, his log might be cut into quarters, each then sawed from the heart lengthwise to the outside, revealing slim wavy pith rays like watersilk ribbons, the thicker lines resembling tigers' stripes, both highly prized. This wood is well worth the additional cost from repeated operational handling with the further advantage of less warping and width shrinkage. Known as "quarter-sawed" the name indicates the resulting rays rather than the method of cutting. Quarters could also be cut diagonally, depending upon desired grain effect.

Our first American frontier settlers, concerned as they were with shelter and survival in the 17th century, had only the basics − benches, beds, and chests, for instance. By 1725 generally improved living conditions plus immigration of expert joiners and carpenters brought about woodworking specialties, objects cleverly handfashioned by using tools. A settlement was lucky to have a resident Cooper (whose craft dates back to 70 A. D.) making essentials as boxes, barrels, churns spoons, and such with a little furniture if they could get ahead of the pressing orders for necessities. Once in a while the head of a household made his own furniture, which accounts for the primitive looking pieces still occasionally seen.

Oak is odorless. With direct steam it was easily carved, pressed, and curved. Metal dies were used under pressure to make the popular pseudo-carvings, especially done on chair headpieces. Oak could be fashioned right from the drying kilns. Though White Oak is the finest, most varieties qualify in varying degrees to their individual purposes. Lumberman and furniture makers had always tried to use White Oak sparingly, but the earliest rich timber stands could not forever handle the onslaught of requirements in the "Golden Era of Manufacturing." Subsequent trees were not so fine a quality.

With long-reigning Walnut overcut by the 1880's, Oak activated by the heady purchasing power of the Vitorians climbed through the 1870's into first place where it continued until around 1930. In trying to conserve, Oak itself began to be used more often as ornamentation on other woods; more abundant and less costly woods began to be backs, drawerbacks, sides and linings, and hidden frames and legs supplementing the Oak principals.

Backs were commonly rough and unfinished; Elm and Hickory were among the substitute woods. Interestingly, it is entire pieces now so treasured. Pine was first used in our American colonies as a secondary wood, comprising backing shelves, lids of chests, and table tops, wherever the strength of Oak was unnecessary. Ash, a little lighter in weight and color, ranked second in value to Oak. Having an even wider usage range, its second growth was applicable as its first, particularly if the tree had rapid growth. Ash rings are wide and regular with broken lines. Oak has a less pronounced grain and more broken lines, and being fast growing, its rings are wide apart. Sharing equally with the Oak in timber classification, the lightweight Chestnut, very susceptible to powder-post beetles, in the 1870's was devested by an Asian blight, pushing Oak one step more as the "Ideal" of furniture manufacturers. Being to the eye,well constructed, and moderately priced to fit medium incomes, Oak became the conventional furniture for the "Middle Class."

MAKING

There were objects manufactured from the original timbers, massive, profusely carved, and lavish with gingerbread details, and often handwork touches. They were expensive then, and they are now. Clinging as they did to Victoriana, when that elegance ebbed, the furniture styles simmered down into plainer lines with fewer and more subdued embellishments. Quantities and urgencies for delivery of orders and shipping charges were necessarily evolved into standardization of styles and, as much as possible, good shipping sizes.

The most sought after finish was and remains "Golden Oak" in full bloom by the turn of this century. Successive layers of hard orange shellac with pigment as yellow ochre, if desired, was put on the whiteness of Oak, each layer allowed to dry; the final rubbing produced the glow. Oak is coarse-grained, and the large pores retained deeper color variations not evident in attempts at falsification, which ended up as uninterestingly dull, solid yellowish-golden surfaces. Many deeper tones were used in stains, not to be overlooked when shopping: silvery sheen, nut-browns, and a ruggedly-weathered appearance. English Oak is darker, often mistaken for American walnut. Despite the individualism of natural Oak graining, Oak was sometimes painted for many reasons: to brighten a forlorn homestead, to cover up wear and aging, and maybe because "they"simply liked it better that way.

Not so popular was the fumed finish, a process used by makers of Mission Oak furniture, and Hubbard and Stickley, who were mindful of the southwest and California Spanish Missions. When using oil base stains, it was unnecessary to come into direct contact with the wood. Therefore, pieces of light wood sealed in an airtight room were darkened by fumes of ammonia set out nearby in open containers.

False graining isn't new. It has been used for centuries. Our craftsmen, imitating Oak and other costlier woods, chemically stained varieties as soft maple and basswood (poplar in Ohio). To help detect this, look on the opposite side of a door, for example, to be sure the natural grain continues on through the wood.

Veneers can be trimmings or completely cover the tops or fronts of furniture surfaces and drawers. Veneers are replaceable if they have become split, broken, or "raised up." They may be personally replaced, glued on without too much trouble with proper guidance, or done professionally. In further efforts to conserve the Oak, manufactures began to use lamination on drawer fronts and table tops, for example. John Henry Belter was a distinguished name among private furniture makers in the 19th century. In 1865 he patented a process of steamheating thin sheets (4 to 16) under pressure in order to better carve stronger furniture. Famous for his grape carvings, he worked principally in rosewood but did use a certain amount of Oak. Furniture never became too splendid for the luxury-loving Victorians.

SALES

Merchandising by retailing mail order houses such as Sears Roebuck, Montgomery Ward, Eaton's in Canada, and The Larkin Co. in Buffalo made everything available to even the most remote regions through tempting illustrated catalogs. First sent by the supplier to local agents for uncrating, any needed adjustments, and delivery, pieces were soon sent directly to customers. Gustav Stickley sent out literature that sowed the seeds for future "do-it-yourselfing." Manufacturers kept busy trying to fill orders, and factories were springing up all over the country. Grand Rapids was endowed to the extent that much 19th century furniture became known then and since as "Grand Rapids Furniture."

VALUES

Age can be noted wherever 19th century craftsmen handcut their dovetailing. Factory dovetailing was precise, more numerous, and all regular — pins the same size as the tails. One factory style resembles scallops with center dots, as when the scalloped hightop edge of a child's shoe of that era was buttoned over the straight – cut edge.

While it is best, of course, to have original pulls and knobs, if they are ugly from rust, missing, chipped, or bent, etc., good replacements are obtainable, and in most cases, preferable for overall appearance. If you are puzzled when buying, and replacements or restorations of any kind are not already tag–marked, ask questions.

Backs are darker from years of constant exposure to air, and if placed in a kitchen adjacent to a cookstove, could be discolored by fumes through the years. Drawer backs and outer sides can be darker since there is air space between them and the cased furniture frame, as opposed to lighter insides of drawers and cupboards or desks protected with closures.

Signatures and other touchmarks, along with original paper tags, labels, brass plates, and especially rare dates command premium prices, as do original furniture pieces fully decorated with clawfoot legs, clutching iron, glass, wood balls, and patterns of carved or applied factory machined flowers, urns, oak and holly leaves, foliage of tracery vines, cherubim, scrolls, dragons, lions' heads, dogfeet, and many other fanciful imagining. Also desirable are labeled plain or partially plain objects which began to appear around the 1870's and were produced by dedicated craftsmen striving for moderation.

It is highly unlikely there will ever be an absolute standardization of prices on this or any other collectible, for beyond the facial elements which vary with the individual dealer and buyer (travel expenses to procure, changing economics, possible transportation costs, local interest, availability of the item, age, workmanship, completeness, and so on) is desire to possess and affordability. A lot to think about in contemplating a purchase but worth it. Like the land, there won't be any more earlier Oak originals. Values given here are what price tags specified. They could range a few dollars less in a lightly populated area or more where demand is greater. Finally, they are definitely meant only as guides pointing in the direction of values with the hope, too, that this book will help identify furniture objects heretofore passed by.

After the 1930's (when parlors stuffy with full-hung wall impediments emerged absolutely plain, when 8-pc. sets of linens like tea napkins replaced those of 6 and 12), popularity of Oak furniture as it had been presented for so many years, fell as fast as it had surfased. Referred to as "you're keeping THAT old stuff?" or "Second Hand Furniture," it has been intensely revived by those seeking heritage and good well-built American furniture that seems to adapt to any other decorative environment. It is easy to "live with".

NICE TO KNOW

Oak is too often regarded synonymously with Victoriana, when actually, its various parts have all contributed to survival and pleasures of man and beast since time began. Children even made toys from the tiny acorn cups. Aside from Victoriana, Oak was the favorite in Medieval Europe, almost stern and barbaric as compared with existing flowing classical lines. It was in heavy usage in 17th century Jacobean England during the reigns of the Charles and James I and II, ca. 1605 – 1686, and Cromwell's time, expressing supreme elegancy of forms.

Types of stools and benches were customary meal-table seating. A wainscot chair with a cushion easing the hard Oak seat probably held the head of the family, befitting his status. Prior to the 1600's, chairs, a symbol of riches and authority, could only be occupied by nobility and office holders. All others sat on stools, benches, or on the floor. Here the first trestle table to be used as an "eating table" was made of a huge Oak tree which supplied the wide plank. In olden times they were known as "Table Boards" and "Oaken Boards." Oak tree bases were often in demand for huge grain mortars; the pestles were large blocks at the end of long handles, which performed as pounders.

"Cuppeboardes, " originally shelves or portable boards for service, were also used literally to store and display "cups." They went on to become enclosed cabinets (cased pieces) with solid wood or glass doors or both. The first mention of this "Cuppeboardes" was in 1344.

And with one Oak stool herein combined with bamboo, did you know that earlier maple was turned and its rings stained to look like Japanese bamboo? It was quite realistic.

And nice to know about clocks...the "Oaks" or "Kitchen" clocks were popular from the 1890's to about 1915. Large companies made them, Ingraham topmost among them. Seth Thomas, Waterbury,

Ansonia, New Haven, Welsch, and Sessions are all well known makers. They were substantially made, about 23" high with 8-day long wearing striking movements. The origin of the embossed Oak is not definite. It was probably kept misty by mold and embossed-die makers, many of those in business around Cincinnati, Ohio. From 1899 to about 1905, figures and buildings were popular and placed at the top middle front. Ingraham incorporated an arm-navy line with doves for Peace, Dewey, Lee, the Maine, and so on. The National line was replaced with subjects as the Old Oaken Bucket for Freedom, Mt. Vernon, etc., while in 1903, other companies featured Teddy Roosevelt and a River line, to mention only a few of the innumerable motifs.

In 1861 William Morris, the English Craftsman and Reformer, deploring factory machined furniture production, began to emphasize, instead, hard work and handcrafting. Not very acceptable at home, he nevertheless was an inspiration for the Arts and Crafts Movement in America from about 1882 until the beginning of World War I in 1914. L' Art Nouveau was the French Arts and Crafts Movement, expressed in the whole leaf and flower forms of nature, even the stalks, as decorating themes. This was very "big" in Europe by 1900 but not overly acclaimed in America. Meantime, about this same period, the English Charles Locke Eastlake felt it personally imperative to instruct the "Colonists" in taste, manners, and their furniture styles. To that end, in 1866 he wrote and published "Hints of Household Good Taste" and in 1872 "History of Revival of Gothic Furniture," although never himself manufacturing furniture. IN 1875 the Mott Iron Works of New City built a castiron sink to Eastlake's design. His efforts are well known and not difficult to recognize once they are pointed out. Perhaps it is one of the easiest styles to identify, having delicately shallow plain or gilded incisings, sawtooth cuts, and overall reduced ornamentation with usually teardrop pulls, brass, and/or ebonized. Their buying public ever avid for "something different." American manufactures literally pounced upon these new ideas with gusto. In fact, enthusiastic manufacturers began not only to build from Mr. Eastlake's designs but extended and expanded them to their own interpretations far beyond their original unencumbered lines...to Eastlake's utter dismay. There was always, however, a final definite similarity among his pieces, and today they remain "Eastlake Furniture" despite their additions.

Gustav Stickley, like Morris, disapproved of Victoriana in general, especially appalled at the vast quantities of furniture produced with factory machining and to him their extreme embellishments. Plus he didn't at all care for the stylized plant forms of L' Art Nouveau. His "words to live by" were "Functionalism" and "Comfort from Simplicity." In 1900 he produced his own interpretations of what furniture should be at his Syracuse, New York shops. He was imitated by many other sources, among them Elbert Hubbard in Roycroft, New York, and his brothers J. George and Leopolc competing with him from their Grand Rapids, Michigan establishment. All of these, along with Morris and Eastlake, were distinguished names in American furniture history. Briefly, theirs were simply old non-violent rebellions against the immediate existing conditions and their zeal for change...in this case against overwhelming and sometimes uncomfortable furniture styles.

Gustav Stickley is attributed with the name MISSION styles; he advocated Oak wood with square lines, wood seats, flat slats, and loose cushions. (His ideas represent the appealing efforts of newcomers to the old Spanish Missions in the Santa Fe, New Mexico regions. Related Ranch pieces of California and the Southwest displayed similar lines.) They additionally utilized longhorn range cattle horns for chairs and tables with Oak and Pine braces or frames just as rams' horns were ages before principally used for the arms of chairs.

Changes are always imminent with tomorrow being contemplated today. Those innovators led the vanguard of a furniture revolution. The very people who had embraced effusive Victoriana in its extremities were wearying of all the pomp and circumstance and expense and were happily ready to accept its erosion into a more relaxed lifestyle. And so that is what happened, while the Oaks bided their time from where they had been stashed away.

So much remembering can be tiring, and there really wasn't much chance, he thought, of any small Acorn being able to direct his own future, but he could influence it by taking that first healthful step toward growing into another grand White Oak Tree; going to sleep! And so, as the forest stilled, he did.

Benches and Stools

BENCH
ca. 1860. Once comfortably enhanced a Judge's Chambers at Martinsburg, W. Va. Courthouse; quartered and plain cut. 11'3" long, 40" high, seat 18½" deep.

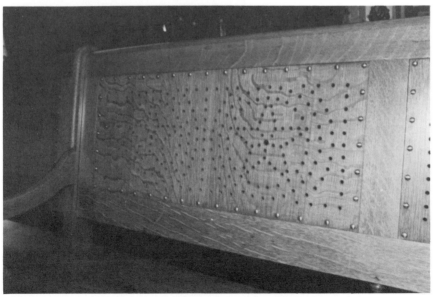

Closer look at punched stars in center of circle designs, eight units, two on each of two long veneer set-in panels on both sides of the center armrest, totaling eight stars in all; slightly slanted back. $1,475.00

L&N RAILROAD DEPOT WAITING ROOM BENCH
ca. 1800's. All original; "wagon" green paint, cast iron fittings; two wood strips beneath for luggage; comfortable-for-backs-of-knees front roll; tongue-and-groove slat joints; marked: DM 2872. 7'4" long, 15" deep seat. $675.00

BARBERSHOP BENCH
Once in a small 1800's Tennessee town to convenience waiting customers; ca. 1880 – 1890; separated slats with a front knee-roll; repainted to original white. 7' long, 36" high. $275.00

14

BARBERSHOP BENCH
For waiting customers; original black leather sections in good condition; ca. early 1900's. 68" long, 39" high; Seat 17" from floor. $295.00

CHURCH PEW
ca. 1920. Plain cut. About 48" long. $425.00

15

BENCH
Texas origin; wide front apron; slanted back; from an old church. 10' long, 33"
high, seat 19" deep. $295.00

BENCH
(As seen in shorter versions on trolley cars); by a center device the adjustable
seat –back can be reversed to enable seating on either side; the construction
is reminiscent of neophytes at early California Spanish Missions, but theirs
had stationary backs; this open – back style is also typical of 18th century
French Canadian pieces in the lower St. Lawrence region; thought to have
emerged in this case from a Railroad Passengers' Waiting Room at a Depot;
long carved settees could also be seen in the early 1900's at New York City
Subway Stations for the convenience of tired folks waiting there to board
commuter trains. 9'5" long, 37" high, 17" deep. $795.00

SETTLE
High back kept off the drafts; note construction. 5'4" long, 44" high, 17" deep.
$675.00

BENCH
Overall uniformly rounded
corners. 7'5" long, 38" high,
seat 10" deep. $350.00

BENCH
ca. 1840 – 1850. Heavy legs through surface are wood pinwedged at a center slash, typical primitive hand – construction. 5' 4" long, 22" wide. $550.00

WASHBENCH
ca. 1890's. Held water buckets or tubs; nut-brown stain. 47" long, 18" wide, 18½" high. $145.00

18

PIANO BENCH
ca. early 1900's. Lifttop with two divided music storage spaces; very heavy. 33" long, 14½" wide, 20¾" high. $145.00

RAILROAD AGENT'S STOOL
Revolving seat; bentwood ring firming splayed legs also provides footrest. $145.00

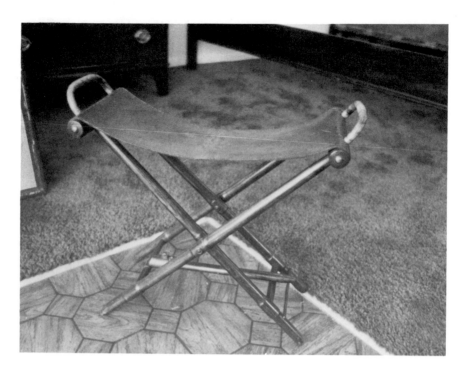

FOLDING STOOL
Oak with brass ferrules; bamboo handles; leather seat. 17" high, 7" wide seat.
$95.00

STOOL
Entirely pegged and glued; ca. late 1800's, "their family's Uncle Brice made it in Tuscarora County, Ohio"; seat curves to unusual comfortable higher-in-the-back-of-the-seat; he wanted a graceful-look; repainted to original white. $95.00

Bookcase & Desks

DESK
ca. 1870. Carved; note eyes and general facial expression differences; dark stained; inside are decorated-arch pigeonholes and writing surface; four long drawers; ornate Victorian. 44" high, 44" wide, 30" deep. $1650.00

STEPBACK STACK BOOK-CASE

These useful pieces from the early 1900's have again been spotlighted by practical furniture buyers; made in individual sections that nest for arrangement at desired levels-can be one high or two low bookcases; wood-framed glass doors are raised to slide back on rails; easy to transport and to "change the furniture around again." 66½" high, 33½" wide, 9½" deep at upper section, lower section is 14" deep. $950.00

STACK BOOKCASE

Quarter-sawn wood; Golden finish; brass knobs; gallery rail around top. 43" high, 34" wide, 13½" deep. $450.00

DROPFRONT BOOKCASE DESK
Stacks; plain and quarter-cut wood; Golden finish; brass fittings. 58½" high, 33½" wide, 12" deep book sections, desk stack 14" deep. $875.00

STACK BOOKCASE
ca. 1910's. Three tiers; plain and quarter-sawn; brass knobs. 44" high, 34" wide. $650.00

DESK, (Office Type)
ca. 1920's. Pullout shelf for typewriter;   Golden finish. $325.00

STACK BOOKCASE-DESK
Dropfront that can be locked at the top; leaded glass panel; brass knobs; lions' feet; today being used as a china cabinet.
$850.00

STACK BOOKCASE-DESK
Unusual with dropfront writing panel having applied carvings; brass escutcheon decorated and protected keyhole; one glass front that lifts and slides back on a rail in top of the shelf; four brass pull-down drawers below; a narrow cornice shelf with gallery across the back; Golden finish; quarter-sawn. Approx. 43" high, 34½" wide, 13½" deep. $895.00

SECRETARY-BOOKCASE
ca. 1800. French Revival influence; unusual double beveled mirror, drawer dovetailed four corners; shallow pigeonholes and dropfront writing surface; Golden finish on plain and quarter-cut wood; elegance in Oak. 66" high, 49½" wide. $850.00

LADIES' DESK
Concave rolled dropfront; gallery edges cut jigsaw type; applied factory machined carvings; locks. 51½" high, 26¼" wide, 16" deep. $450.00

LADIES' DESK
Dropfront: round beveled gallery mirror; bowfront drawer; brass fixtures; plain and quarter cut. 44" high, 24½" wide, 14½" deep. $395.00

LADIES' ROLLTOP DESK
ca. 1870's. Nut-brown stain;
self knob and pulls;
unusual. 43" high, 31⅜"
wide, 22½" deep. $650.00

**LADIES' DROPFRONT
DESK**
Original key; dovetailed
drawers four corners;
recently painted white with
pulls and incising darkly
accented. 37" high, 25" wide.
$195.00

S-ROLL DESK
ca. 1910. A "handy" smaller size not often seen; vertical base panels; locks; Golden Oak finish 47" high, 42" wide, 30" deep. $1,750.00

S-ROLL DESK
These rolltops "are supposed to" slide easily (and good old ones still do), made of thin parallel slats fastened horizontally to a flexible backing. 44" high, 47½" wide, 30" deep. $1,100.00

PARTNERS' DESK
Double deep, of course; both sides same fittings; drawers, doors, brass key-hole-lock escutcheon; ledger-file compartments behind doors; dovetailing; plain cut and Tiger Stripes. 31" high, 54" wide, 36" deep. $1,600.00

ROLL DESK
ca. 1870. Paneled back; cherry-color stain; pullout shelf each side; wood draws, brass inside knobs; top can be locked (closed). 44" high, 48" wide, 28" deep. $2,250.00

CLYINDER ROLL DESK
ca. 1870. Golden refinished to original; plain and quarter-sawn; bow and panel lines with brass pulls (draws). 42½" high, 37½" wide, 21½" deep. $1,275.00

PANEL TOP DESK
Slanted top folds at center and is raised back; beveled (chamfered) panels and door; all original. 50" high, 50" wide, 30" deep. $1,425.00

STICKLEY DESK
ca. 1910. All original; now rarely found, particularly in this fine condition; label on bottom of drawer; QUAINT FURNITURE CO., STICKLEY BROS. CO., GRAND RAPIDS, MICH. Company owners, J. George and Leopold, were competitive brothers of of Gustave Stickley; spiral twist legs; wood-framed finely-caned panels each side; table-length drawer with self-wood knobs, generous lower shelf. $1,300.00

MISSION TYPE DESK
Veneered top; base shelves each side, 28½" high, 42" wide, 25½"deep. $325.00

CHILDREN'S TWIN DESK SET
ca. 1930. Divided table sections, individual lift-up tops; nut-brown stain; attractive simplicity. Desk closed: 24" high, 36" wide, 13¾" deep. $175.00. Chair: 28½" high; Seat: 14" high, 12" wide, 13" deep. $40.00

CHILD'S DESK
Step-top; wide wood pulls with underside fingers-grips. 24½" high, 30" wide.
$225.00

CHILDERN'S SCHOOL DESK
Double desk with inner divider and individual lift and work surface top;
continuous seat and back, iron frame. 30" high, 40" wide, 14½" deep. $165.00

Cabinets & Cuboards

ENGLISH HOME BAR CABINET
Now waiting in Tennessee for an American residence; ca. 1875; the dark Oak finish was stripped and Golden Oak added; leaded clear glass with sides and center stained glass areas on the front and smaller units at each side (wouldn't a tube light hidden back of the droop frame to shine through be beautiful!); shelves, posts, drawers, mirrors; hooks at open ceiling holding glasses ready to be used; mint condition; setback top; fully dovetailed drawers; quartered and plain cut Oak; wide cornice. 84" high, 60" wide, 22½" deep. $3,200.00

KITCHEN CABINET
ca. 1880 – 1890. Refinished light nut-brown; complete as original with exception of restored porcelain knobs; random width back boards denote early piece; has a flour bin, wide work surface, spice drawers, "storage and show" behind glass, short turned legs (Alabama origin; type legs often seen on southern pieces), designed pediment; possum belly drawer at left bottom stained to simulate the wood. 75" high, 48" wide, 28" deep. $1,275.00

DRY SINK BAKER'S CABINET

ca. 1870 – 1890. Dough roller board when not in use is raised to make a closure for the open shelves, fastened with a catch; paneled construction; black iron fixtures; pullout bread cutting board (or to set things on) between sink and top of left lower door, the right a pullout bin for sugars, meals, or such; table flatware and spice drawers with three on right rear base side for towels and miscellaneous; rare pulldown flour bin behind left long narrow door; wells often metal-lined so dishes could be washed in a dishpan; called "dry sinks" because they were not connected to a pump or did not have a drain. $975.00

"HOOSIER" CABINET

So-called as a style made and popularized in Indiana (the Hoosier State); pullout metal flour storage bin with sifter in bottom; roll-up door hides shelves; top glass panels are etched; white porcelain work area. 69" high, 41" wide, 26" deep. $975.00

36

KITCHEN CABINET
Zinc top work space. 68"
high, 42" wide, 24½" deep.
$395.00

BUFFET
Oval front, flat back; plain
and quarter-sawn; Empire
Revival influenced with side
posts of the beveled mirror
and the front overhangs at
the top of the middle-con-
cave-carved front uprights;
factory dove-tailed drawers;
Golden finish; shelves held
treasure along with the top
except when the latter was
needed to hold serving
dishes; fretwork on the glass
doors. 51" high, 45" wide, 21"
deep. $895.00

CHINA CABINET
Plain cut, Tiger and quartersawn wood; convex sides glass side columns; four inside shelves; beveled gallery mirror molding framed with applied (wing) corner carvings; decorative posts; original key; short cabriole legs with claw feet; casters. 72" high, 44½" at widest part; mirrored gallery 42½" wide, 12½" high; all as original. $2,250.00

CHINA CABINET
Mirror inside back reflects displays; flat back; adjustable glass shelves; cornice; dogs' feet; plain and quarter-cut wood finished Golden. 65" high, 49" curve. $2,900.00

CHINA CABINET
Plain and quartered finished Golden; three adjustable glass shelves; mirrored inside back; dogs' feet with metal casters; graceful base finger rolled. 87" high, 43" wide. $1,350.00

CHINA CABINET
Curved convex glass; quartersawn; marked: "Berkey & Gay, Grand Rapids, Mich;" leaded design. 58" high, 34½" wide, 13" deep. $750.00

CHINA CABINET
Front panel replaced. 57"
high, 39" wide, 14½" deep.
$250.00

CHINA CABINET
ca. 1920. Even the inside
shelf backs are quarter-
sawn; three convex glass
panels; Empire influence,
casters. 60" high, 42" wide,
15" deep. $875.00

CHINA CABINET
ca. 1890. Quarter-sawn; Golden
finish; strange heads, claw feet;
veneered roll; gallery. 59½"
high, 42" wide, 14" deep. $895.00

CHOCOLATE (PASTRY) CABINET
While most were imported from Holland, this is quarter-sawn, Golden glow-
ing American Oak; lift-off tray for serving; the (porcelain) servers (Limoges
here) were kept conveniently inside (and for "show"); square brass pulls let
down beveled glass doors held by two chains each; once in fairly good supply,
these cabinets are now harder to find. 28½" high, 24¾" wide, 16¾ deep. $850.00

CURIO CABINET
One large glass door; three
shelves. 48" high including
½" high gallery at back, 23"
wide, 11½" deep. $250.00

TEACART
Removable serving tray; Golden finish; casters. 27" high, 27" wide, 17½"deep.
$495.00

PIE SAFE
Never as plentiful in Oak as Poplar, pine, and walnut, and more; paneled each side; tins punched "in" making outside surface smooth, a more quality method; two inside shelves; dovetailed drawer four corners. 49" high, 33" wide, 14"deep. $795.00

KITCHEN OR PANTRY CABINET
Inside shelves handy for storing tins and other cooking utensils; fit limited space. 74" high, 23¾" wide, 25½" deep. $375.00

CABINET, INCUBATOR FOR BABY CHICKS
Now an interestingly novel table for many rooms in a
home; drop-front panels; side tin water and feed cups. 30"
high, 28½" wide, 28¾"deep. $225.00

SMOKERS' CABINET
1920's – 1930. Copper lined interior; shelves each side; turnings. 28" high, 29½ "
wide. $155.00

44

CORNER CABINET, HANGING
Quarter-sawed; one inside shelf; 20" across. $175.00

SPOON RACK
Bottom storage drawer; holds 12 spoons; early "heart" eye for hanging. 18" high, 4½" deep, 11" wide. $255.00

FIRELESS COOKER

Original label: IDEAL FOOD COOKER; low shelf ; metal fittings aid in moving about and front fastener hold lid down tightly; each of three separate lids has a steam-vent hole; three inside deep, round, fully metal-lined compartments held special-size food containers with lids (not now present). Stones originally sized to fit were heated and placed beneath the pans to generate the heat for cooking. Light brown stain. 34" high, 43½" wide, 15" deep. $895.00

DENTAL CABINET
ca. 1880's. Rich nut-brown tones;
handwork; original glass knobs
with one replaced; upper right
pullout shelf; two top doors
swing out to the left; small,
medium, and large drawers with
a one deep door compartment;
vase molding; inside dividers;
refinished. 54½" high, 23¾" wide,
cabinet 12" deep with top 13"
deep. $1,175.00

DENTAL CABINET
Quarter and plain cut; various
sizes storage compartments; white
china knobs; slim reeded pillars at
mirrorsides; nut-brown stain; all
original. 6' high, 34" wide, 12"
deep. $1,100.00

DENTAL CABINET
Quarter-sawn; Golden finish; frosted glass under top panel that lifts and slides into concealed grooves; brass pulls; two "secret" drawers under removable milkglass work surface; all insides of drawers are Birdseye Maple; marble base; conveniently galleried top shelf. 54" high, 36" wide, 12¾" deep. $1,295.00

CABINET
A marriage cabinet (see Glossary) ca. 1890 – 1900; bookcase set on a chest; two top drawers can be locked; black iron hardware. 74" high, 40½" wide, 20" deep. $525.00

ICEBOX

Chestnut and Oak; zinc lined; pull-out panel at base to empty drip pan; tongue-and-groove wainscotting paneled back; frequently made of Elm or Ash. While so many of the old Oak collectibles are today extensively reproduced, iceboxes are especially so. 42" high, 35" wide, 18" deep. $600.00

ICE BOX

A cased piece; restored and refinished marble replacing inside zinc; four panel sides. 41½" wide. $675.00

ICE BOX
"Gibson's Cambria;" front-top iron lift handle; ornate hinges. 43" high, 25" wide, 18" deep. $550.00

REPRODUCED ICE BOX
Top lift handle center of door; shiny brass fixtures; "White Mountain." 39" high, 21" wide, 18" deep. $295.00

ICE BOX
On brass plate: WINDSOR; refinished; pull-out bottom panel for emptying concealed drip pan. 49" high, 25½" wide, 17½" deep. $550.00

CABINET
ca. 1910. Paper label on back states definitely "ON LOAN to consignee for the exclusive sale of Belding goods and could be recalled at any time." 37" long, 36½" high, 17" deep. $475.00

CHEST
For small tools in engineering and machining; Golden finish on plain and quarter cut; brass fittings; leather carrying handle. 13¼" high, 19¾" wide, 9" deep. $195.00

CHEST, MEDICINE
(Can hang) Plain and quarter cut, brass knob. 19" high, 15" wide, 6½" deep. $95.00

FILE CABINET
Two deep drawers; brass
fixtures; two-panel sides,
28" high, 14¾" wide, 17"
deep. $110.00

DOCUMENT BOX
ca. mid-1800's. Quarter-sawn, Golden finish; top center beveled
panel; brass hinges; dovetailed four corners; satiny patina. 9½" high,
30½" long, 17" wide. $295.00

FILE BOX
Four dovetailed corners; lift top; label: "WEIR CO., Monroe, Mich., Made in U. S. A." $45.00

FILE BOX
Brass catch; beveled panel on lift-top. $75.00

Chairs

ARMCHAIR

Once a Senator's Chair at the old State Capitol in the Senators' Meeting Room at Jefferson City, Missouri during the last quarter of the 1800's. Grecian style, cabriole front legs; one incurred stretcher has two spooled angled rungs firming it into heavier plain splayed back legs; cushioned slipper feet; saddle seats; deep stained brown; all original. Seat 20" wide at front, 14" wide at back, 19½" deep. $795.00

ARMCHAIR

Colonial revival, ca. 1890 – 1900. Plain and quarter-sawn; Golden finish; finely carved finals; knuckled and parchment rolled handrest and the same type parchment scroll on the rolled-back crest. (Egyptian and Greek mythological themes and constructs ideas frequently appeared on 19th century pieces to about the turn of the century.) $525.00

ORNAMENTAL ARMCHAIR

Eclectic with Empire Revival; deeply carved scowling Gargoyle with a very long tongue; scrolled, scalloped ears and fierce mustachios; rolled handrests; quality spool and bulb turnings on front stretcher; delicate French Baroque cabriole front legs (style that originated with the Chinese, used on late William and Mary style furniture, and appeared in the 1600's on some Flemish Pieces); plain or carved; in usage for over 50 years on Louis IV and V furniture; Chippendale, Georgian, and Queen Anne wrap around arms interrupted by high back with crest and stayrail pattern molded; from placement of the rear legs it was a CORNER CHAIR, but probably had usage wherever needed; three tuned underside rungs. 44" high. $975.00

56

RECLINER (MORRIS CHAIR)

ca. 1800's. All original with Golden finish; hoof feet. (Egyptian and Grecian Revival construction and others of their features continues throughout the 19th century.) William Morris, English craftsman, to name one of his many careers, was most uncomfortable on Victorian chairs. So about 1860, trying for "adjustable comfort," he brought out "easy chairs" having an iron rod resting in a slotted projecting rear rack, this holding the hinged chairback in any of, usually, three to four positions. 40½" high, 31" wide, 39" deep. $675.00

RECLINER (MORRIS CHAIR)

ca. 1890 – 1900. Five side baluster spindles; Golden finish; reupholstered; patterned heavy front supports continue into base scrolls; casters; adjustable iron rod. 38" high, 27" wide, 28" deep. $675.00

RECLINE (MORRIS CHAIR)
ca. 1900 – 1910. Golden finish; iron rod; chairs constructed of flat-sawn boards; originally sold inexpensively. 38" high, 27" wide, 28" deep. No cushion yet. $525.00 as is

ARMCHAIR
Stickley Bros. put a red paper label on inside of chair apron: STICKLEY BROS. CO., GRAND RAPIDS, MICH., MADE FOR REVELL & CO., CHICAGO, ILL, FUR-N I T U R E - R U G S - DRAPERIES; and added their gold and black label on the opposite inside: QUAINT FURNITURE, STICKLEY BROS. CO., GRAND RAPIDS, MICH.; chair all original as found and shows the seat caning; spirals; small ball feet; flat back panel and each side "butterflied" out; wide rolled-under hand rests. $900.00

ROUNDABOUT CORNER CHAIR

Could also have been used as a Desk or Occasional Chair; seat replaced; wide fretwork slats with armrest resembling Chippendale; this type customarily fabric upholstered originally. (With a low two-front-sides apron concealing a chamberpot, this was a general style of chair used as a "Closestool" in 1700's New England, its slipseat easily removed.) $575.00

ROUNDABOUT CORNER CHAIR

Midwestern origin, Quaker type; bentwood wraparound; the whole chair was originally stained black; 19th century corner chairs are very rare, making this a unique one. $495.00

59

BEFORE – AS FOUND

Stickleys added two red paper labels, one on each underside of the aprons; QUAINT FURNITURE CO., STICKLEY BROS. CO., GRAND RAPIDS, MICH.; the other, MADE for REVELL & CO., CHICAGO, ILL., FUR-NITURE-RUGS-DRAPERIES; the original caned seat was replaced with closely-fit wood slats; plain and quarter-sawn, spirals, and fine-canned framed partial splat; note narrow flat rails stub-projecting beyond front and back feet at either side. $795.00

AFTER – RESTORED

WINDSOR

Again illustrating that the Oaks were not limited to elaborate Victoriana. A Hoop and double Hoop-Back Windsor; deep saddle seas; rolled under knuckle handrests; White Oak; all original. First made in America by 1725, they were named for the town of Windsor, England in their district of origin, 165th century. In the mid-1800's they were smothered by Victorian "fancy" chairs, as Sheraton, for instance, and heavily-factory-produced Captains' Chairs. Pictured here, the spindles go through the arm; they are also known as STICK CHAIR. Prices not available on these two items not comparable would have to be excellent and start about $975.00

CAPTAIN'S CHAIR
ca. 1850 – 1870. Victorian era; A Captain's Chair means one with arms a continuation of the back, clear around from the first to the last of the eight spindles; saddle seat. 31½" high, 18½" wide, 18¾" deep. $195.00

ARMCHAIR
Lacy double caning restored; bowed arms with notched handrests; baluster stiles; pleasing back framing. $250.00

ARMCHAIR
Quarter-sawn veneer head-
piece; plain veneer seat;
Country style; bentwood
highrise arms; S-curved
back, and fastened to seat;
tall finial. $195.00

CONVENTIONAL CHAIR
Seat replaced; Golden finish.
Many manufacturers turned
out endless quantities. 37"
high, 19" wide. $135.00

DESK CHAIR
Quarter-sawn; revolves all the way around; new leather seat; adjustable height, tips back; casters. 36½" high, 19¼" wide, 18" deep. $195.00

DESK ARMCHAIR
New seat; flared arms; 11 spindles. 40" high, 22½" wide, 18" deep. $225.00

ARMCHAIR
Writing arm; slatback; hand-fashioned; from a rural Georgia school. 34½" high, 16" wide, 15" deep. $150.00

ARMCHAIR
Handmade during the 1800's in Missouri; slatback; rush seat; (low side stretchers indicate rockers were then usually added to an existing straight chair); the first rockers were short, extending the same distance from the front as from the back legs (interchangeable, actually); rockers kept growing longer at the back, which is one way to help date them. 43" high, 20¾" wide, 16¾" deep. $350.00

ARMCHAIR
Golden finish; pressed splat, headpiece, and front; annuletted; seat fabric to be furnished. 38" high, 26¼" wide. As is, $195.00

INVALID'S CHAIR
Chestnut; pressed back drop door affords access to underseat box for chamber pot; its rolled rim secure on wood rails; two fingerholes in lid. 42" high, 21" wide, seat 18½" deep. $195.00

CHILD'S FLIPSEAT CHAIR ca. 1900. Underseat label: STREIT MFG. CO. CINCINNATI, O. SHAKESPEARE CHAIR; 30" high, 17" wide, 15" deep. $85.00

CHILD'S EARLY CHAIR Handmade slatback; from the mid-1870's until after 1900, this furniture was copied from "Mayflower" (Pilgrim) styles having both wood pegged (pinned) and mortise joints and tenons that "stuck outside" their posts. (A very similar type reflects southwestern ranch pieces. Much reproduced.) $55.00

67

CHILD'S TRAINING CHAIR
Jigsaw cutout splat; apron above button feet conceals space for chamberpot; lift-top in seat. 35" high, 35" wide, 19" deep. $225.00

HIGHCHAIR
ca. 1920's. For dolls, with
tray, 28½" high, seat 10"
deep, 11¼" wide. $150.00

HIGHCHAIR
For older child, never had a tray, sometimes called Youth chair; pressed back;
rolled arms, five spindles with ring turning, two each side. 42" high. $225.00

ROCKER
Seven turned spindles (matching three at each side) separate wide top and slat, both elaborately pressed with (pineapple) centers; seat restored to original. 42" high, 18½" wide, 17½" deep. $350.00

70

ROCKER
Quarter-sawn and plain with curved-down veneer seat; 11 back spindles, three each side set into heavy turned stretchers; might indicate rockers added later to a straight chair; Golden finish. 38½" high, 20" widest part. $350.00

ROCKER
Golden finish; pressed head-piece; arrow-back slats; four turned spindles each side; early rolled-under arms fastened in this manner to the seat are of Pennsylvania origin. 40" high, 21½ wide, 19½" deep. $350.00

71

ROCKER

ca. late 19th century. Arches and spindles reflect the Spanish Revival influence, while the shape of the carved oak leaves and acorns headpiece suggests adaptation of the Boston Rockers, these last, however, customarily with one arch each side; the general standard headpiece style on many chairs after 1830; medallion seat; turning and bowed arms with front posts having a matching ball underseat; whorl-foot rocker fronts, curled up, typical of "Victorian"... or, as some pieces are called, "French Revival Antique." 43" high, 19½" deep seat. $425.00

ROCKER
Reupholstered seat; Mission type square construction with shaped splat. 37" high, 26" wide. $195.00

ROCKER
Molding on front of rolled down veneer seat; 37½" high, 20½" wide, 21" deep. $175.00

ROCKER, NURSING OR SLIPPER
Pressed back with tiny buttons top; bentwood braces; high grove–and–ball–finials; nine spindles. 42" high, 20" wide, 28½" deep $325.00
(Slipper chairs existed in the 1600's with fine examples popular during Queen Anne's early 18th century reign; conveniently low seat for ladies to don their slippers.)

ROCKER
ca. 1890. Cut-out back quarter-sawn veneer; seat plain veneer; flat lightly base-craved slats are set in the side stretchers, appearance indicates rockers were added to a straight chair; the rolled under seat front is nicely molded; ornately "country." 39" high, 20" wide, 21" deep. $295.00

ROCKER
Golden finish; plain and quartered; restored caned seat; beading and Oak leaves pressed back. Sometimes a NURSING ROCKER with comfortable splayed arms to rest the adult's arms; the side post and balusters are set back so baby could be laid across the lap without bumping its head 37½" high, 19" wide. $250.00

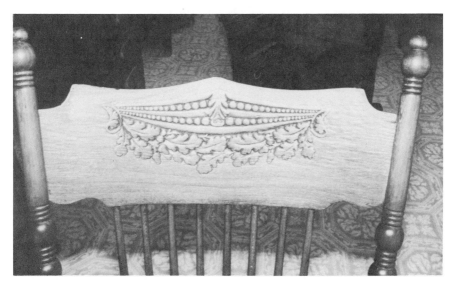

ROCKER

ca. late 1800's. Three cross-pieces with matching pressed patterns; Golden Oak and some Chestnut; new leather center seats; curved-down armrest curve high to brace higher than usual on stiles; prominent finials. 40" high to topmost, 20½" wide, 18½" deep. $225.00

SEWING OR NURSING ROCKER

Refinished to original Golden finish and seats re-eye-caned; seven spindles with interesting tiny ball turnings while three front stretchers are sausage and bulbs; medallion shaped seat; factory carvings, beading, and scrolls; bentwood back braces are attached to the seat. 38" high, 17½" wide, 17½" deep. $295.00

SEWING ROCKER
Partitioned drawer pulled out from underseat storage with knob; Golden finish; saddle seat. 33½" high, seat 17" wide, 16" deep. $145.00

ROCKER
Painted wood, pressed paper seat replacement; splayed spindles. 40" high, 17½" wide. $125.00

Before – As found

To match the straight chair of the same design, this also carries the company name and Made for Revell information on one underside apron while the opposite side is the gold and black Quaint Furniture identification, and as always, their trade mark. In this instance, the center panel has been recaned to the original; the cushioned seat above the caning now showing the slats replacement, the cushion to the taste of the purchaser; short rocker projection at the back. $825.00

After – Restored

Both are Oak with walnut arms; ca. 80 years old; flat shaped spindles; restored woven seats; acorn-without cup-finials. $250.00 each

ROCKER (GRANDPA'S)
42" high, 28" wide, 17" deep

ROCKER (GRANDMA'S)
42" high, 25" wide, 17" deep

ROCKER
Dark stained overall; original Oak splints; side stretchers wood-pinned to outer side of splayed legs; saddle seat. 40" high, 31" wide, 19" deep. $225.00

ROCKER
Pressed and scalloped one-side back crosspieces with seven grooved and spooled spindles, similar trims on stiles; eyecaned seat; all original. 38" high, 18" wide, 15" deep $195.00

ROCKER, PRIMITIVE COUNTRY STYLE

Entirely stained black; while these shaped slats are characteristic of French Canadian furniture, this was 19th century handfashioned miles away in Mississippi; woven splint seat replaced; note now the arms are supported by projecting short horizontal posts, and the dowel-rod-type rails holding the back stiles to front uprights, fastened on each outer side, these matched by the back crossrails on either side of the lower slat to the high back; rockers put on with the post-and-socket-method; most 19th century stretchers go unto the posts, not through them. 42" high, 19½" wide, seat 20" deep. $265.00

ROCKER

Mission type; original leather; deep stained. 32½" high, 26" wide overall. $250.00

REPRODUCED CHILD'S ROCKER
Purchased by a Missouri dealer who can easily properly position the arms, which the manufacture put on backwards; then he can sell it with that amusing information on the tag; pressed back with split buttons, a fan, and much more; front seat skirt; Golden finish, substantial. $85.00

CHILD'S BENTWOOD ROCKER
ca. End of 1800's. Hand-made, Kentucky origin. $125.00

CHILD'S COUNTRY STYLE ROCKER
Very wide headpiece, and arms are high on the posts; no evidence it ever had spindles; heavy construction; stained pecan brown. $125.00

CHILD'S ROCKER
Wide bowed arms; cameo shaped back; the original veneer removed from it, and new replacement veneer applied, ready for the whole chair to be refinished nut-brown or Golden to taste; illustrates how sometimes replacement enhances the appearance of furniture when veneer, as here, was badly broken. As is $50.00. Restored $95.00

ROCKER
Windsor type with standard
(Boston) type headpiece;
Golden finish. 39" high, 25"
wide. $295.00

ROCKER
Fretwork, factory headpiece
with design carrying out
overall general design;
unusual ovals have been
added to extend narrow
straight armrest; quarter-
sawn; Golden finish; needs
new seat. 33½" high, 26½"
wide, 24½" deep. $175.00

ROCKER
Shaker type finial ovals;
slatback; plain and quartered; handfashioned; rushes
woven seat. 43" high, 20¾"
wide, 16¾" deep. $150.00

PORCH ROCKER
Slats construction; double
front stiles braces each
side. $150.00

PLANK SEAT TAVERN OR HOME CHAIR
ca. 1850 – 1875. Nut-brown stain; when legs were extended through the seat as here, the legs were split and top wood-pin-wedge in the manner of the first Windsors. 37½" high, 16½" wide, 16½" deep. $225.00

PLANK SEAT TAVERN OR HOME CHAIR
ca. 1850 – 1875. Oak and Pine; ball turned legs; heart cutout. 37¾" high, 16¾" wide, 16½" deep. $225.00

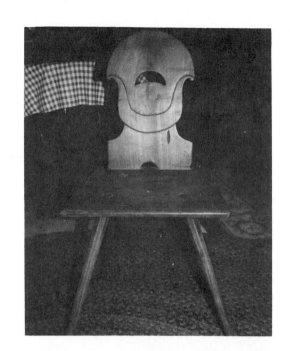

PLANK SEAT TAVERN OR HOME CHAIRS
ca. 1850 – 1875. Oak and maple; always the back cutout slot. 33⅓" high, 17¼" wide, 15" deep. $225.00

87

PLANK SEAT SIDE CHAIR
ca. 1850 – 1875. Oak and
Pine incised pattern on
seat; iris carvings on both
sides of the back; (the
pineapple, American Colo-
nial emblem of hospitality,
and the heart, were the earliest and topmost designs);
heart cutout here. 34" high,
14½" wide, 15½" deep.
$395.00

PLANK SEAT SIDE CHAIR
Oak and Pine; turned legs;
rose carvings both side of
the back, also showing back
construction joining into
seat; heart cutout; incised
pattern on the seat. 33½"
high, 14½" wide, 15½" deep
$395.00

TAVERN (PUB) CHAIRS
Quarter-cut veneer seats; refinished; loop-back center backs; a unique feature is that the loop firming the legs is fastened at the inside of the front two, carries across the sides openings, and is bent to be screw-fastened to the insides of the rear legs about 4½" from the floor. 34" high, 14½" seat diameter. $125.00 pair or $125.00 each

TAVERN (PUB) CHAIRS
Low back; plain veneer seats; bowed top rail scrolled under. 30" high, 14" seat diameter. $225.00 pair or $125.00 each

SIDE CHAIR
Illustrating the notched finial greatly used in Spanish southwestern furniture, here beaded-and-leaf carved; roundels and clover crest; deep stained; many 19th century revival adaptations. Price not available-comparable price $750.00 minimum

"KITCHEN WINDSORS" SIDE CHAIRS
Loop-back; as original. It was one of Sears "Special Leaders" in their 1897 catalogue listed also for Dining Rooms, a "first-class chair" in bow-back three spindles style, finished plain, dark, or antique; with plain spindles it cost 34¢ or $2.00 for a set of six; for 38¢ each or $2.20 for a set of six you could have the "fancy" (meaning grooves on the rails and stretchers) version. 34" high, 14½" wide, 14¼" diameter seat. There are only three chairs available – so – $55.00 each

CHURCH CHAIR
Hymnal box on back. 33½"
high, 13¾" wide, 13½" deep.
$95.00

Shop Tag specified: ENGLISH SCHOOL CHAIRS. Also seen in earlier rural
America as CHURCH CHAIRS; school book (or hymnal) box on back; rush
seats; 3" wide top rail all original. 32½" high, 16" wide, 15" deep. $295.00 for set
of four

CHILD'S PRIMITIVE CHAIR

Handmade; splint seat; all original from 1860; (these are heavily reproduced in varying touches and finishes); curved horizontal flat bowed rails. 20" high, 13½" wide, 11" deep $75.00

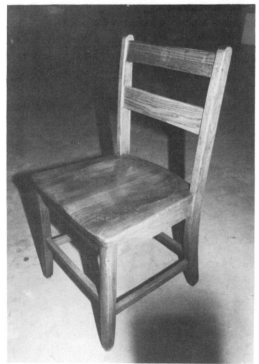

CHILD'S MISSION TYPE CHAIR

Mildly-saddle seat. $45.00

SIDE CHAIR

Patent dated on seat back: 1866 and 1870. It is unusual to find such a design from 19th century America; the underseat strengthening and heavier wider seat frame hoops were made from Oak under direct steam, bent, and "V" end fit together, as a mortise and tenon joint seen on wooden buckets and measures; three arrowback slats with feather cuts visible only on the outer two; Loop-back adaptation of Windsor. $250.00

CHAIR

11 short spindles divide deeper stained-trimmed oval back; leather seat; short back on higher base denotes a Vanity or Ladies' Desk Chair, but with three for sale they were probably a dining set. 37" high, 16½" wide, 17" deep. $125.00

94

DINING CHAIR
Golden finish; Butterfly (or Angel) Wing deeply pressed headpiece and bell center pressed seats design; these quality features along with so many varied type turnings on so many rails (13) are uncommon, indicating careful workmanship. Such examples create interest in and appreciation of American Victorian Oaks. Headpiece: 6½" high, 21" wide, seat 16½" wide, 15" deep. $275.00

DINING SIDE CHAIR
Leveled with a rubber cap on rear leg; would be pretty and not difficult to replace the seat and refinish Golden. As is, $50.00

SIDE CHAIR, REPRODUCTION
Faithfully detailed to originals; looks new beside the old. $100.00 each with any desired number available

DINING SIDE CHAIR
Pressed back; spindles divide floral and beading patterns; note that stiles on most of these dining chairs of the Victorian period are "fanned out"; braces and high finials in manner of Rodback Windsors. 36½" high, 16" wide, 16" deep $225.00

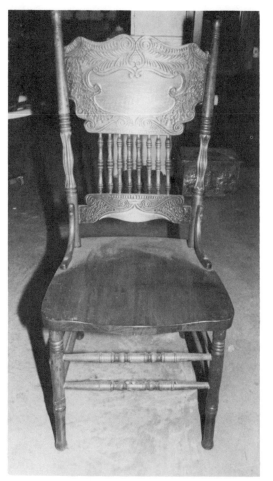

DINING SIDE CHAIR
Eight spindle deeply molded wide headpiece with plain medallion center (which always seems to me ready for the family crest or initials added as on silver); style is an offspring of early Winsor Rodbacks, very poplar around the finials; fluted and "New Spool" turning (since the 1830's). 36" high, 15¾" wide, 16" deep. $225.00 (dust included)

DINING SIDE CHAIR
Center pressed back seat replaced; eight windsor type spindles; braces. 44" high, 18" wide, 16½" deep. $150.00

DINING SIDE CHAIR
Six plump turned spindles;
scalloped and pressed
stayrail and headpiece;
Rodback Windsor adapta-
tion; braces. 36" high, 16"
wide, 16" deep. $200.00

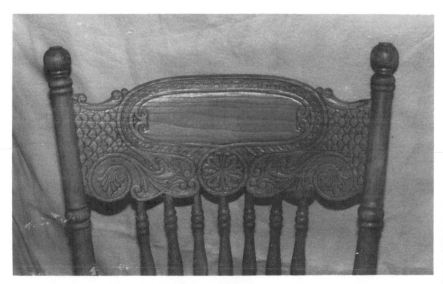

DINING SIDE CHAIR
Restored caning; birds' wings pressed pattern. $125.00

DINING SIDE CHAIR
Rodback Windsor type; pressed back; six spindles. $175.00

DINING SIDE CHAIR
Original leather. 38" high, 19" wide, 17" deep, $600.00 set of six

SIDE CHAIR
Cut-out splat; top turned rail makes convenient carrying device; reupholstered seat. 41½" high, seat 16¼" x 16¼". $195.00 pair

DINING SIDE CHAIR
Headpiece pressed border; caning
replaced. $125.00

DINING SIDE CHAIR
Golden finish; rolled-back top
stiles; seat needs replacing; low
stretchers. 42" high, 17½" wide,
16½" deep. $125.00

Bedroom Items

WASHSTAND-COMMODE
Towel bar; tilting mirror;
applied machined carvings;
Hotel type. 72½" high, 40"
wide, 19" deep. $650.00

WASHSTAND-COMMODE
ca. Nineteeth century. Wishbone holding towel bar; hotel type; skillfully carved; all original; closer views to better see brass draws and details. 58" high, 34¾" wide, 17½" deep. $750.00

COMMODE
Three-panel sides; nut-brown stain; self-wood knobs; drawer has four-corner factory dovetailing. 23¾" high, 32" long, 17" deep. $350.00

COMMODE
(Washstand-Commode) Original ornate brasses; wide splashback. 28" high, 29½" wide, 15" deep. Hanging mirror above: 24" x 15"; sold as a set of two pcs. $375.00

COMMODE (Also Washstand-Commode)
ca. 1880's. Typical usage was to store porcelain chamber sets (or occasionally metal pitchers and bowls); Eastlake influence with incising; darkened brass pulls and brass-and-ebonized knob; wood escutcheon; side-braced splash-back. 34" high, 26" wide, 18" deep. $395.00

COMMODE
Refinished Golden; casters. 24½", high, 32" long, 17¼" deep. $245.00

CHEST
ca. 1930. Chestnut classified with Oak in our collectible; ca. 1930; elaborate brass pulls; factory dovetailed drawers and Golden finish. 36" high, 38" wide, 14" deep. $295.00

CHEST OF DRAWERS
Bowed veneer fronts; brass pulls; modified cabriole feet. 40" high, 30" wide, 19" deep. $350.00

MATCHING DRESSER AND WASHSTAND SET
Both pieces have the year 1903 stamped on mirror backs; veneered drawer fronts; hardware replaced; rare mirror moldings. DRESSER: 80" high, 44" wide, 21" deep; WASHSTAND: 76" high, 33½" wide, 18½" deep. $1,900.00 for the set

DRESSER

All original; Victorian Renaissance flavor in heavily carved front feet and elaborate pediment; top two drawers bowfront; mirror stiles are columns supporting a scrolled-ends horizontal column; wing–shaped carved back braces each side; from an Alabama home of the last century. 85" high, 50" wide, 24" deep. $850.00

DRESSER (BUREAU)

Four dovetailed drawers, the two smaller can be locked; brass fixtures; Golden finish. 70" high, 40" wide, 18½" deep. $395.00

DRESSER
Five dovetailed drawers; applied carvings; grooved pediment stiles with ornate finials. 81" high, 48" wide, 22" deep. $495.00

WISHBONE DRESSER
(Sometimes "Lyre")
Named for the curve of
beveled mirror's carved
arms each side; Golden finish; paneled sides. 75" high,
42" wide, 21" deep. $250.00

BUREAU
Tiger Stripes; beveled early
type mirror; reflects Empire
Revival; drawer fronts dovetailed. 48" high, 66" wide, 23"
deep. $295.00

CHIFFONIER

ca. 1920. Wishbone (or Harp) style with beveled mirror; veneered; serpentine (swell-front) drawers; Golden finish; brass escutcheon protect and embellish keyholes since each drawer can be locked; applied factory-machined carvings. 69" high, 32¾" wide, 19" deep $395.00

CHIFFONIER

Wishbone; mostly quarter-sawn; dovetailed drawer fronts; Golden finish; casters. 59" to shelf, 23" more to mirror top, 32½" wide, 19" deep. $395.00

LINGERIE CHEST
(Also described as popular with gentlemen for small clothing; shaving supplies kept in door compartment). It is RARE. Applied carvings; plain and quarter-sawn wood; Golden finish; brass fixtures; scalloped base skirt; fully dovetailed drawers. 56" high, 26½" wide, 17" deep. $850.00

DRESSING TABLE (Later a VANITY) and CHAIR SET Table has adjustable side butterfly beveled glass mirrors; casters; Empire influence; bowfront veneered long top drawer and straight across smaller ones; wood knobs; both pieces plain and quarter cut. Table: 29" high, 16" wide, 14" deep. The set $365.00

BED
Factory machined carvings and moldings applied both ends; panel trim; complete; full size. 78" high, 56" wide. $550.00

BED
Golden Oak; many have the panel back type construction, some also on the footboard; pressed pattern with pointed arches over flowered branches; heavy gracefully applied machined carvings and moldings as well. 79" high, 56" wide. $650.00

116

BED
With slats; "blanket roll" baseboard; Oak dark stained; applied leaves, scrolls, and flower carvings; panel construction both top and baseboard. 78" high, 56" wide. $575.00

BED
ca. 1890. "Blanket" roll at top of headboard and footboard; paneled trim; applied deep factory carvings. 73½" high, 56½" long, 56½" wide. $475.00

118

BED
Rails included; refinished Golden to original. 39½" high, 55" wide. $150.00

DOLL'S BED
ca. 1900. Slats construction; dropside. 22½" high, 27¼" long, 15" wide. $95.00

BAROQUE BED AND BUREAU (DRESSER) SET

Plain and quarter-cut wood, finished Golden; the wide top panel of the bed is veneered; ornate shell crest on each with various other applied carvings in shells, leaves, and scrolls, along with beading and cameo patterns; animal feet, blanket rolls bed top and bottom and a Bureau cornice; many rounded columns; these pieces should not be moved for photographing due to limited shop space, but their handsomeness is still clearly evident; note the molded convex front of the two drawer, both four-corner dovetailed; brass pulls; the huge beveled mirror denotes a nineteenth century Victorian manufacturer. Bed: 86" high, 59" wide; Bureau: 89½" high, 51½" wide. $2,400.00 for the two pieces

ARMOIRE (WARDROBE)
All original; three shelves
inside; dovetailed drawer
corners; glass is beveled;
Tiger Stripes on posts with
some areas quarter-sawn in
slim rays; impressive shield
and top corners; mid-nine-
teenth century. $1,250.00

WARDROBE (CLOTHES-PRESS)

Gradually evolved into a clothing storage furniture piece from the "Ambry" which was originally used to store ancient "arms"; applied single flower top front corners; molded cornice; base drawer; (no key but keys can often be found at flea markets); paneled sides; horizontal reeds. 72" high, 43" wide, 16" deep. $475.00

WARDROBE

ca. 1890. These were known as "Portable;" plain and quarter-sawn with one lower right side panel of door having Tiger Stripes, unusual; applied floral carving at door to curve; brass escutcheon and ornamental knob; ca. 1890. 72" high, 35½" wide, 15½" deep. $475.00

Hall Items

HALL TREE

"Hour-Glass" shaping like fashions of the day. Also called Stands, Racks, or Benches; fashionable and functional; a wide range of styles and sizes; popular, especially through catalogue advertising; this had applied carvings and pediment; natural color iron ring at right side to hold parasols (or umbrellas); hooks; quarter-cut wood Golden finished; lift-top covers space for items such as overshoes (and when top was down, made a seat for struggling them on); a "fancy" piece. 78" high, 25" wide, 14½" deep. $645.00

HALL TREE

Victorian; quarter-sawn and plain; beveled glass mirror; hooks; bowed arms. 80" high, 32" wide, 11½" deep. $395.00

HALL TREE (RACK)
Applied carvings; hooks; bowed
arms and lifttop; fashions influenced "wasp-waist;" all original.
78½" high, 27" wide, 15" deep.
$795.00

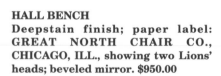

HALL BENCH
Deepstain finish; paper label:
GREAT NORTH CHAIR CO.,
CHICAGO, ILL., showing two Lions'
heads; beveled mirror. $950.00

Music Makers

ORGAN
VIOLA; STOREY & CLARK, CHICAGO, U.S.A.; dated inside case: 1843; golden
finish; beveled mirror and all complete as original, also operable incised
designs, gallery rail ball turnings; candle/lamp shelves; high bricabrac shelf;
foot-pedals fold into base; paneled keyboard closure; quarter-sawn and plain
cut; it is uncommon to find these old organs made from Oak since most were
walnut or cherry. 72" high, 52" wide, 22½" deep. $1,650.00

MUSIC BOX
Pat. dated: Dec. 11, 1889 and June 27, 1893; trademark has foliage, a lyre, swan with outspread wings; brass plate: "REGINA #61505;" 12 steel records, all pat. dated; brass fittings-lid fastener; removable wood-handle iron crank fits round slot inside box; scenic paper liner; woodpinned corners; complete and operable. 7½" high, 12" wide, 9½" deep. $1,250.00

ORGAN VOCALION
ca. late 1800's. Vertical panels halfback to shelf; plain and quarter cut; each side has candle or lamp shelf. 80" high, 70" wide, 32" deep. $1,795.00

126

PIANO STOOLS

Most follow a same (or similar) general style and size with individual variations in finishes; turned or reeded (both combined here) splayed legs; larger center posts, and sometimes seat-edge grooving; each has brass claw-and-glass-ball feet; revolving seats for up or down adjustments on metal stems; heavily reproduced item. About 19" high with 14" seat diameter. $125.00

127

PHONOGRAPH
On brass label: HIS MAS-
TER'S VOICE; complete
and operable, has needles,
crank, and records; chrome
fittings; red tin Morning
Glory horn mouth diameter
19". $700.00

PHONOGRAPH
Brass label shows: THE
ELEPHANT BRAND TALK-
ING MACHINE along with
picture of (small) elephant.
Horn mouth diameter 16½".
$725.00

Country Store Items

SEEDFRONT COUNTER
Counter-wide deep bins opening at the back (displays at front behind glass); paneled ends; all original. More than 10' long. $1,300.00

COUNTER
In service over a hundred years in an Elm Tree, Missouri general store; note large roundels and the variety of patterns. 8' long. $1,200.00

RIBBON CABINET
Six Tiers; glass front doors lift up to slide back out of sight rails; pullout sliding side "shelves" hold stocks back of front display row; from the last general (country) store to go out of business at Smyrna, Tennessee. $995.00

SPOOL CABINET
Four drawers and mint leather center of lifttop; refinished Golden as original; dull brass pulls. 30½" long, 11" high, 22½" deep. $675.00 with table (sewing machine base)

130

CASH REGISTER
Marked: **DAYTON, OHIO U.S.A.** Lever opens divided-sections drawer which automatically locks when pushed shut; tape for registering sales brass fittings. **$975.00**

BUTTER CHURN, BARREL TYPE
Could be purchased at general stores; one side hand-crank intact, the other lost; White Oak staves tightly grooved together (but additionally, the moisture in the milk expanded the wood so the casks didn't leak); churn could be simply rocked back and forth, or much more vigorously, turned over and over, end for end; maple "stand;" iron fittings; lid fit securely as slots on churn rim held the iron bar curves, clamped with the center gadget. 16" diameter, 32" high. $375.00

BUTTER CHURN
Complete with inside windmill paddles that can be lifted out. $225.00

Sideboards, Servers, and Buffets

SIDEBOARD
Solid wood and veneer;
principally Tiger Stripes;
unusual placement of mir-
rors; S-bowed base doors
and drawer; two drawer"
under platform are "bow-
front"–which, more often
tan not–is a veneered bow;
wood pulls; animal feet;
weighs about 250 pounds.
82" high, 49" wide, 13" deep.
$1,025.00

SIDEBOARD
Serpentine drawer front quarter-cut veneer; applied fancy foliage carvings;
brass knobs and pulls; bow-legs with dog feet; interesting handling of woods
on two drawer fronts; beading; top is corniced. Low Server height of 40", 44"
wide, 21½" deep. $395.00

SIDEBOARD
Maker French influenced as L'Art Nouveau type applied carvings; acanthus, foliage, and scrolls; beveled shelf-divided mirrors; each storage compartment can be individually locked; brass fittings; Golden finish; broken pediment with pretty center and molding. 82" high, 60" wide, 22" deep. $1,000.00

SIDEBOARD
ca. 1870. Massive carvings and bowfront areas; Golden finish on mostly quarter-sawn; raised panels; beautiful carved pediment with beading and roundels, having a rare center insertion of a Tiger roll; note typically generous mirror; brass pulls; animal feet; pillows and shelves; found in Virginia. 82" high, 54" wide, 23½ deep. $1,200.00

134

SIDEBOARD

Handsomely carved with lions' paws as feet for both the cased piece and its arched lions' body posts; drawers four-corner factory dovetailed; plain, quarter, and Tiger Stripes wood; Golden finish; lions' whiskers, teeth, et al. are finely done, and it is highly unusual to see the open mouth of such a lion with it realistically-sized tongue hanging DOWN as here. Until the close of Word War I mirrors were generously proportioned with large reflecting areas; afterwards, they became smaller and ornate framing became quite plain. 80" high, 60" wide, 24" deep. $2,850.00

Five Views of SIDEBOARD ca. 1800's. Magnificently embellished; Golden finish; plain and quarter-sawn; Details: Old Man of Mountain (looking almost benign) and fiercer lions' heads with scrolls and moldings; applied carvings; brass knobs and lions' mouth pull; all original. $1,295.00

SIDEBOARD
ca. 1900. Empire style;
Tiger Stripes; large mirror.
60" high, 60" wide, 27" deep.
$795.00

SIDEBOARD
Tiger Veneer and plain cut;
mirror replaced; flower
shaped and cared stiles. 77"
high, 45½" wide, 21½" deep.
$495.00

BUFFET
Solid and quarter-sawn wood in Golden finish; wood
knobs; parchment scrolled feet. 38" high, 42" wide, 19"
deep. $350.00

BUFFET
ca. 1920 – 1930. Quarter-sawn drawer veneers; pressed front molding. 40"
high, 44" wide, 20" deep. $595.00

BUFFET
Tiger Stripes veneering; square wood pulls; year 1916 stamped on back of mirror. 52" high, 46" wide, 20" deep. $595.00

COVERED BUFFET
(A rarity!) ca. 1900. Golden finish on quarter-sawn wood; realistic animal's feet; brass draws; the horizontal "butterfly wing-shaped" beveled mirrored gallery extends into side mirrors while the all around molding drops from the top to each glass base side forming one (bird's) wing; door and drawers compartments held linens, silver, and dishes; the glass panel was lifted to slide back on rails under the buffet top, protecting goodies (as cakes and cookies, fruit, pies, custard, and the like) on the felt covered shelf from flies and other obnoxious flying intruders. 59½" high, 44" wide, 20" deep. $1,250.00

SILVER TABLE (SERVER)

ca. 1920's – 1930's. Plain and quarter-cut with Golden finish; two side drawers while one at center raised top slides forward, having divided spaces for flatware; bulbous top; finger roll size grooving on legs; antiqued brass loose drop pulls. 29" high, 41" wide, 20½" deep. $275.00

SILVER TABLE (SERVER)

Plain and quarter-sawn; lined silver flatware drawer; storage space each side; square Mission lines but softly grooved moldings and patterned brass pulls keep it form austerity; unusual. 31½" high, 28½" wide, 17¾" deep. $250.00

Table, Stands, and Pedestals

DINING TABLE SET
Table has two extra leaves for center pullout insertion, held by wood pins set in socket joints on the matching width; plain and quartered panels form the surface; the large square-cornered base is solid Tiger Stripes wood; heavy platform having animal feet; brass scatters added sometime after origin; nut-brown Table: 3½' high, 44" top diameter, six chairs, each: seat 17½" high; veneered; pressed seat centers and backs; eight short back spindles, turned; factory applied wings carvings. $1,300.00 set

DINING TABLE SET
One extra board; quarter and plain cut; feet claws are prominent. Table: 29½"
high, 48" top diameter. $895.00; four chairs: 39" high, 16" wide, 16½" deep. $185.00 each

DINING TABLE SET
ca. 1900 – 1910. Four board table extension. Table: 30½" high, 38¾" long, 37" wide. $575.00; Four Chairs: 36" high, 12" wide in front, 16¾" deep. $125.00 each

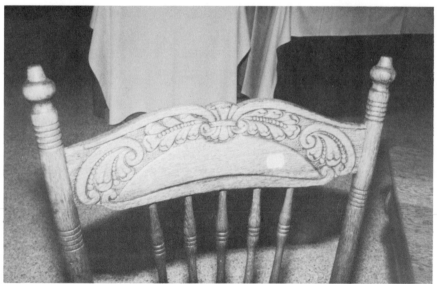

DINING TABLE SET
Tiger Stripes; squared edge bulbous legs; four side chairs; pressed head-pieces; five turned and grooved spindles and two tall finials. Chairs, $125.00 each; Table, $550.00

DINING TABLE SET
Set up with its four extra removable (any or all) boards (leaves); massive lions'
feet legs; there are seven chairs plus host's armchair. Table: Set up 95¾" long, 48"
wide, 29¼" high. Chairs have been leather re-covered at center seats. Note mythi-
cal grotesque face at top of chair splat. The set is priced at $2250.00.

145

DINING TABLE SET
Partially quarter-sawn; Golden finish; four angled (gateleg-type) table supports joined at a center split post for handling a two-leaf opening; cushions tied-on over original leather seats; hoof feet at front, plain splayed below slantbacks. Table: 29½" high, 42" top diameter. The set with four chairs, $900.00

DINING TABLE
Nut-brown stain; one extra leaf; four chairs available. Chairs: 36" high, 17" wide in front, 16¾" deep. $125.00 each. Table: 29½" high, 42" diameter top. $595.00. Small wood basket on the table with bentwood handle is valued at $22.00

DINING TABLE
ca. 1880. Tiger Stripes; lions' feet with well defined carvings; "feathers" on legs; ever so many Empire Revival features used in Victoriana; very large round post. 31" high, 54" diameter top. $875.00

DINING TABLE
Two extra leaves stored in well under top; fifth leg goes under at center and while available, dealer had not yet had time to put on; corner applied carved shields; onion footings and at top of stubby, chubby legs. 29" high, 48" sq. top. $895.00

REPRODUCED CHILD'S PLAY DINING SET
Doll size; four spindle-back chairs; made by a craft shop in natural Oak to be refinished as desired. $150.00 for the set of five

COUNTRY KITCHEN TABLE
Chestnut; turned and fluted four corner legs and the fifth at center. 30" high, 42" long, 27" wide. $295.00

TABLE
Handcrafted; to quote Dealer: "Nothing standard about it – it's even 2" higher than customary;" top consists of blocks reverse-grain, set into pine reinforcements beneath; thistle-type feet complete ornate legs; two top sections can be pulled apart to accommodate extending table with a 15" wide center board. 37" high, 54" long, 41" wide. $695.00

TABLE (Bible Stand)
The type that often held the Stereopticon and its box of views; delicate style not indicative of its sturdiness; patterned four-sides valances match the wings holding legs off from shelf; turnings on legs. 28" high, 21" sq. top. $295.00

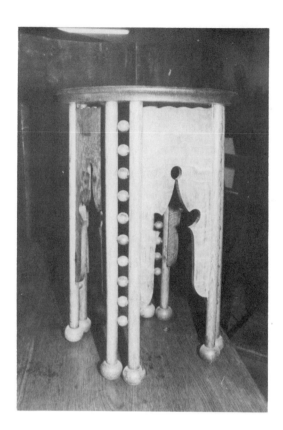

JARDINIERE STAND (TABORET)
Very fancy with cutouts, ball turnings; imaginative maker; a pale Golden finish and plain and quarter-sawn. 20¾" high, 13½" diameter top. $195.00

STAND
Often used in bedrooms; button and bulb turnings; Golden finish with a scalloped-edge shelf; cornice-slanted table surface. 29½" high, 16" square top. $125.00

PARLOR TABLE (or STAND)
ca. 1880. Scalloped edge surface; flat button turnings. 28¾" sq. top. $165.00

BAKER'S TABLE
(POSSUM BELLY in many areas, especially the Midwest)
Golden finish; two deep curve-bottom "Possum Belly" bins painted to simulate natural wood grain; once contained flour, meal, etc. 30" high, 46" wide, 25" deep. $475.00 (Saw one almost identical in another shop at $500.00)

SALESMAN'S SAMPLE TABLE
Quarter and plain cut; note cornice-top inslanted fashioning; husky ball turnings; mint. 18" high, 16" sq. top. $295.00

SALESMAN'S SAMPLE TABLE
ca. 1800's. Quarter and plain cut; Golden finish. 18½" high. 14¾" dia. top. $225.00

LIBRARY TABLE
Handsome ornate trim; grooved side aprons; rope edged shelf; note ends patterns and top-to floor wide shaped moldings. 29½" high, 41" long, 28" wide.
$425.00

PARLOR TABLE
ca. mid 1800's. Fancy leg
turnings; brass claw and
ball feet; beaded carved border. 30½" high, 28" sq. top.
$525.00

PARLOR TABLE
Type used in centers of
room; large cannonball turnings end in brass claw and
glass ball feet, the outside
claw of each having a
grotesque face like a fic-
tional Wolfman with hair-
standing straight up; the legs
are darker; they were habit-
ually cut from the end
grains, absorbing as such,
stains and other finishes
deeper into the wood, 30"
high, 28" sq. top. $425.00

COUNTRY TABLE
Quarter and plain cut;
Golden finish; handtooled
legs have one each leg Old
Spool turning with other
styles above and below it. 29"
high, 23" diameter. $245.00

PARLOR TABLE
ca. 1870. Dark stained; massive post reeded near stylized base serpentine top
edge with narrow apron; at
first glance, a contradiction,
at second glance, a pleasing
medley of styles. $245.00

OCCASIONAL TABLE
Often bedroom used; Chestnut; Florida origin. 29½" high, 22" wide, 19½" deep. $115.00

DRAFTING TABLE
Top briefly slanted up to the rear with storage compartments inside table; top lifts; plump turned legs; partially quarter-sawn and finished Golden. 38" high, 71" wide, 31" deep. $425.00

PEDESTAL

ca. 1800's. Tiger Stripes and plain cut; pressed and molded trims. 33¼" high, 15" sq. top. $295.00

PEDESTAL (LAMP)

Quarter and plain cut; four angled pieces mortised to center post four separate ornate curves from opening and support top; dark stained and heavily embellished. 38" high, 11½" across octagonal top. $295.00

PEDESTAL (BIBLE OR FERN)

Tiger Stripes; scrolled feet and uncommon half-scrolls rolled under each top side of post under a double surface; Empire Revival style. 38" high, 14" sq. top; 5" sq. post base tapering to 4" sq. at the top. $215.00

157

PLANT (FERN) STAND
Brown stained; shaped skirt four sides.
33" high, 12" sq. top. $135.00

JARDINIERE STAND
(TABORET)
Considered stylish ornaments for
any parlor. 17" high, 11" straight
across octagonal top. $75.00

STAND (FERN, LAMP, OR ALBUM)
Narrow pressed apron four sides;
reeded and turned legs; tiny brass
claw and glass ball feet; Golden finish.
31" high, 16" sq. top. $195.00

158

Miscellaneous

PICTURE FRAME
Nut-brown stain, goldleaf band; near-mint overall. 18½" wide, 32" long. $125.00

PICTURE FRAME
Light-stained frame with a darker new molding as original. $95.00

FRONT DOOR
Eastlake motif; shallow incising, reeding, turnings, and applied sawtooth cuts; door awaits replacement of original frosted glass and its original patterned large brass doorknob now being cleaned; from a home in Pensacola, Florida, late 1800's. 82" high, 36" wide. $550.00 complete.

160

KITCHEN MANTEL CLOCK
(or as often called GINGER-BREAD CLOCK--obvious name from ornate decorating); strictly Victorian 1890; even the pendulum is lavish; NEW HAVEN, CONN. 8-DAY; strikes hour and half hour; when new it sold for about $2.00, 50¢ more if you wanted an alarm attachment. $350.00

MANTEL KITCHEN WATER-BURY 8-DAY;
Strikes on hour and half hour; no alarm. $200.00

KITCHEN MANTEL CLOCK
ca. 1890 – 1900. American Gilbert; Spring wind; has alarm; strikes on the hour and half-hour; elaborately decorated, stained in reds and blues with contrasting natural wood tone areas. $350.00

ROUND ENGLISH GALLERY CLOCK
ca. 1860 – 1870. Hanging; works are in the wood box at the top back. $400.00

"POP'S" WALL CLOCK

ca. nineteenth century. Ornately decorated with acorn and ball finials; roundels; elaborate pediment; incised and applied carvings; 30 day-no strike; large brass and wood pendulum; original key and label; Waterbury; Golden finish; is operating as original; second hand, 48" high, 20½" wide, face diameter 12". $895.00

WALL CLOCK

SETH THOMAS, has the rarely-found original key which inserted at the left side, used to open the case and wind the clock; time only; quarter-sawn Golden Oak; Case#2 8–DAY with second hand; refinished. $875.00

WALL CLOCK
REGULATOR marked on front; full case frame, pressed designed; original paper tag on back has "Rules for Setting and Striking," other maintenance instructions along with: "The Sessions Clock Co., STAR (rest of name of clock style torn off) Successors To The E. W. W. Welch Mfg. Co., Forestville, Conn. U. S. A.;" has the original key; fancy brass pendulum on wood strip; brass face ring had to be replaced. 32½" high, 18" wide straight across middle of octagonal top; 13½" face diameter. $475.00

TELEPHONE
STROMBERG CARLSON TELEPHONE MANUFACTURING CO.; the Cadillac of phones; dated on receiver: "Nov. 27 – June 12, 1894 – Rochester;" brassedged transmitter; Tiger Stripes and plain cut. $395.00

TELEPHONE
Double Box type used for Long Distance; marked: "Chicago Telephone Supply Co., Elhart, Ind. U. S. A.;" quarter cut; high shelf for book, writing, or leaning. 32" high, 32½" wide. $350.00

TELEPHONE
Tiger and plain cut; Long Distance calling style; wall hanging. 32½" high, 32½" wide. $350.00

**TELEPHONE
WESTERN ELECTRIC
MADE IN U.S.A. on label;
operated with side crank;
Golden finish. 19" high, 8¼"
wide. $295.00**

**TELEPHONE
KELLOGG, quarter-sawn;
Golden finish; four sides
dovetailed; side handcrank;
operable (terminals made
for present day phone co-
approved connection);
receiver is on upside down
as was often the case with a
housewife rushing to check
oven-baked goodies, party-
line listeners hurrying back
to chores; or talk-ending
just-plain-quicker. 17" high,
5½" deep. $295.00**

MANTEL

Once housed for many years at old Hotel Congress in Niagara Falls, New York; Wood panel at some time replaced; original mirror above arches held by Grecian Ionic-type grooved columns; beveled glass must have once reflected luxuriously gowned ladies and frock-coated gentlemen; Della Roggia carvings of garlands and cameos (influences of American Art Nouveau from the French L'Art Nouveau introduced about 1894). 98" high, 60" wide, 11" deep. $895.00

MIRROR

Awaiting return of its beveled glass which had to be resilvered; satiny patina. 30" high, 33½" wide. $235.00 complete.

MIRROR EASEL
ca. 1888. Back stand folds flat while shelf can be raised with slim brass link chains; mirror partially handpainted. 23" high, 19" wide. $125.00

PICTURE FRAME
ca. 1865 – 1870. Ornate goldleaf designs inside deep stained Oak. 33" high, 29" wide. $225.00

SHADOWBOX MIRROR FRAME
Ornate, inside twisted molding and wide goldleaf; hanging. 15" x 12". $175.00

TRUNK
Handfashioned by a craftsman for his wife in the late 1800's on the lower Niagara Fountier; has a unique brass recessed combination-type lock; beveled (chambered) panels each side. 19" high, 46¼" long, 17½" wide. $425.00

Glossary

Acanthus – Stylized leaf form from southern Europe used decoratively in the 18th century by Robt. Adams & Bros., architects, creating the classical revival style in furniture; Sheraton and others worked in the mode, and it was reactivated in the 19th century for the "Oaks"

Annulet – A small ring; a series of linked or separated decorative circles

Applied – Attached to, meant here as trims; carvings, turnings, etc. attached to a furniture piece

Apron – A trim or structural aid; a skirt, being a designed or plain wood strip at the base of a chair seat, cabinet form, and such; can be used to conceal underframing, etc.

Arrowback – Flattened spindles having arrow-feather or arrowpoint end-shapes; spaced on chairs backs

Barley Sugar Twist – (or merely Barley Twist) Wood turnings imitating the spiraling of barley sugar twists; could be carved or plain spirals

Baroque – Rococo–gaudy–anything over decorated; Second Baroque refers to Victorian usage; the word Rococo as from the Portuguese meaning shells and rocks in decorative patterns

Bulbous – A bulb is a stretcher having an elongated bulb section at the center (as tulip, etc.); Bulbous refers to the rounded section of a turning.

Burl – Abnormal knotty outgrowth on oak, maple, ash, walnut, mahogany, and such hard and semi-hardwood trees; its mottled effect, when thinly sliced, made fine furniture veneers; a wart on a tree – highly prized

Cabriole – Many variations in both legs and feet of furniture; bowlegged (reverse-curved), used in the 1600's and into Victoriana

Cased – Any cabinet-type piece of furniture; enclosed; a place of security for storage

Casters – Small wheels or rollers set into the feet or bases of furniture to facilitate moving it about; can be metal, glass, or wood

Chamfer – Surface made by beveling (cutting away the angle of two pieces of wood); leaves a raised panel; often seen on inside of very early cupboard doors

Circa – About, around the time of; abbreviation: ca.

Concave – Incurring, dished, rather than a swelled front; the opposite of Convex

Cornice – A protecting upper border; an Entablature, the top most section of, for instance, a classic column

Convex – Bulging outward, the opposite of Concave

Crest – The ornamental peak, or top, on furniture; taken from the word describing plumes, etc. at the top of a knight's helmet

Cylinder Roll – As on desks and secretaries, the solid, curved sliding top concealing a writing surface and/or storage; in antiques vernacular sometimes called a Barrel Roll.

Della Robbia – The delicate garlands of flowers, fountains, urns, and such used by the family of this name, beginning in the late 1400's in Florence, Italy. While they usually employed rich colors, these tracery-type motifs are so-called for them.

Dovetailing – Flaring mortise and tenon strong joints resembling a dove's tail.

Draws – Handles, any drawer pulls; originally the drawers themselves were "draws;" (early brass pulls were often called "brasses.")

Ebonize – Staining black to simulate ebony

Eclectic – Choosing from various styles to form or embellish a furniture piece; a combination of several period motifs, not to be confused with a Marriage

Embellish - To adorn; to make beautiful with decorating

Escutcheon – Keyhole plates, decorative and protective, for doors, drawers, and cabinet furniture pieces, in brass, ivory, bone, contrasting woods or an "escutcheon" wood which was holly

Ferrule – A metal (brass or copper) cap, little bracelet, or ring put around something, as tool handles, etc. to prevent splitting and generally strengthen

Finger Roll – Continuing hollowed-out (concave) rolls cut into the margins of chairs, settees, and other furniture items

Finial – A terminal (top) ornamentation, as acorns, balls, mushrooms, figural, and so on; inverted finials are often acorns.

Fluting – Wide round sections in relief as on columns; the opposite of Reeding

French Revival Antique – Actually means "Victorian;" stems from an English Cabinetmaker, Morant, in 1850 seeking to revive the French styles of the Court of Louis XIV; not a very familiar term

Gallery – A low fretwork or solid, practical, and decorative railing around the tops of furniture forms

Gargolye or Grotesque – In regard to furniture decorating these two go together; Grotesque means fantastic or barbaric as distortions of animal or human forms, often set amid greenery, fruit and/or flowers for fanciful ornamentation.

Gingerbread – Excessive, showy

Headpiece – Topmost staysail as on a chair, plain or fancy

Incising – Gouging out, can be deeply cut surface designs

Jigsaw – Open designs, fretwork sawing; done with a fretsaw

Laminating – A process of thin layers of wood (4 to 16) steamheated under pressured for overall greater strength or for more successful intricate carvings; also conserved White Oak by using lesser woods

Marriage – Or Married-Off; elements not originally paired, as chests, cabinets, etc., putting one on top of another to create a Highboy, for instance, traditionally done and acceptable if so indicated to the buyer

Medallion – Curving bands (sometimes called an Eastlake style) and forms; a shield or medal shape

Molding – Shaped length of wood applied as a frame or border; best known are Ogee, Scotia, Cyma, and Ovolo; can be flat or beaded

Pediment – Ornamented structure, molded or other pattern, atop a cased furniture piece; a Broken Pediment is interrupted as its highest point with a separate crest.

Plank Bottom – Any all-wood settee or chair seat

Punched Tins – Best quality in Pie Safe panels are punched from the "outside-in" and nicely framed in the wood; of lesser quality are those punched from the "inside-out," and those which are nailed onto cutout openings on the outer or inner sides of the door.

Reeding – Opposite of Fluting; semi-circular straight cuttings resembling natural reeds

Rolltop – Narrow top-rounded-one-side parallel slats on a flexible backing to be roll-raised up and down to protect writing surfaces and file compartments inside the furniture piece.

Roundel – A furniture term meaning round (circular) ornamentation.

Rungs – Below the seat; rounds of a chair

Serpentine – Wavy (sinuous, snaky) curves of furniture legs usually having a convex center; also noted on fronts of cabinet-type doors and drawers

Slat – Narrow, thin bar of wood or medal

Slipper Foot – Outcurving furniture foot shaped like a lady's slipper toe; seen on both early and late cabriole legs

Splashback – or Splashboard; a high rim or gallery at the back and sometimes also the sides of a bedroom piece such as a washstand, preventing walls from becoming splattered while washbowl was in use; this part being of wood or marble

Splats – Plain, decorated, or cut-out pattern, vertical center piece in a chair or settee back

Splayed – Canted; legs slanted outward for added strength and steadiness, as on a chair to kept it from tipping

S-Roll – Cyma Roll or double curve as a cabriole leg line

Stayrail – Horizontal plain or decorative crosspiece firming the frame, as in a chair back

Stile – The upright elements in a framed furniture piece, as the side supports of a chair back

Stereopticon – Optical instrument for home entertainment; popular Victorian handle-held viewing device with two eyeglass viewers to bring long double scene cards into one large picture, this adjustable to individual distance

Stretcher – Horizontal bracing under tables and chairs (also acted as foot rests)

Tongue-and-Groove – Cut with a special plane which did not appear until the late 1600's; the Plow cut the groove for which the Tongue cut the tenon to fit; more often seen on tables where the extra boards (or one side of the top of those center-jointed table) were extended into the tenon that was cut the width of the board so that it would fit precisely into the other half or grooved section; this particularly used on gateleg and butterfly type tables; it should appear in the construction of those joints on the better 17th century pieces.

Valance – Skirt or apron; designated for the top rather than the base of a furniture object

Wainscot – Solid wood Tudor type chair with a "Wainscot" back; to line or panel walls within wood – "wainscotting."

Whorl Feet – A knurl or curled-up scroll.

Windsor – A spindled type of chair popular in our American Colonies and, particularly, 18th century England

Index

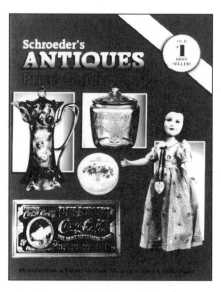